LINDBERGH

An American Epic

by

GEORGE G. COX

THE GOLDEN QUILL PRESS
Publishers
Francestown   New Hampshire

© THE GOLDEN QUILL PRESS 1975

Library of Congress Catalog Card Number 75-22928

ISBN 0-8233-0228-8

Printed in the United States of America

```
PS            Cox, George Gurney
3505
.0962         Lindbergh
L5
1975
811  C839L
```

DEDICATION

To my wife, Lucile Elizabeth Cox, my companion and co-worker for forty-two years

PREFACE

In this poem we discover an amazing accomplishment. Lindbergh is a famous name and personality, but no one has tried, to my knowledge, to put his genius into poetry. His valuable contributions to humanity, scientific and spiritual, deserve an inspired epic such as this.

What the Reverend Cox has tried to do is this: first of all, he lays a groundwork spanning the sweep of the universe's creation, the struggle and progress of life on a planet destined to culminate in one man, and on this canvas, he necessarily has to use history, anthropology and biological development. Secondly, he concentrates on the successful achievement of one man who has been predestined by the Deity to do this upon the stage of the present world. In the awesome expansion of this vision, Mr. Cox attains a feeling of the true epical range that we find in Benét and Whitman.

In the form he uses a variety of meters, free verse, cadences — sometimes a rough pentameter shifting into the shorter rhythms. But the subject-matter always fits the form, and we would not have it otherwise. There are springs of true inspiration and intuition in these lines. He is exuberantly buoyant about his subject and his faith in the Deity. This is something that few poets have dared to attempt. I recall Stephen Benét's *John Brown's Body* as a singular forerunner.

I feel this historical work with its continuing creation, backed up by a divine universal plan, to be excitingly impressive and unforgettable. It gives one unexpected pleasure and I know that many readers will discover in it a world of hope and belief, the like of which has not often been seen before.

—Daniel Smythe

CONTENTS

Gateway	13
A Brief Prelude to Canto One	14

Canto One

The Progress of Man	19
First Interlude	37

Canto Two

Boyhood Days of Lindbergh	41
Second Interlude	47

Canto Three

The Pilgrimage of Peace	53
In Memoriam	64

LINDBERGH
(An American Epic)

GATEWAY

Sometimes you enthrall me, relentless earth,
Bathed in the healthful atmosphere of all living,
And habitation of such human greatness —
Such magnitude of men of science.
Sometimes, again, you comfort me
As in ordered cadence you orbit the sun, —
Ever singing songs of harmony
With other stars and spheres.
And yet, when I see in my amazement
How rapidly you are shrinking
As, year by year,
Those supersonic sounds and sights
Go streaking through the stratosphere,
Exposing quickly all corruption
And all futility of wars,
I grow weary of you.
In retrospect I seek to break
The bounds and barriers of earth
And fly ever upward by
An endless path of stars,
Finding other greater, brighter worlds
To satisfy my questing soul
Until each impossible dream
Toward which I reach becomes a reality.

A BRIEF PRELUDE TO CANTO ONE

From nothingness and always darkness
To light and color, forms and patterns,
From bits and bubbles of floating gases
To spinning forms in solid masses;
From spinning forms to perfect planets
(Sun, moon and earth, and life upon it),
From ages when time was not
To the age when time shall be no more,
And from ocean to ocean and zone to zone
A Master Mind, a Living Spirit,
Who was and is, and ever shall be,
Is ever moving and creating.
A Living Spirit? Yes, and more.
A Music Maker Who goes singing, dancing
Down all geologic ages
By ordered and precise harmonies
In microcosms of living matter,
And macrocosms in solar systems
Of all celestial spaces.
Yes, ever singing, ever dancing
Goes the joyful Music Maker
Up the ladder of all living
From green algae to great redwoods,
From single cells to dinosaurs
And from warm-blooded mammals to
Climbing primates until He reaches,
In the process, His master composition, —
The master plan in the soul of man.
For all intelligence of every soul
Needs to emerge from the Master Mind,

The Music Maker of all living.
And each of us as mind and soul
Must find his vocal key, a unique chord
That is all his own, to play in the music
And harmony of the universe of the Maker.

CANTO ONE

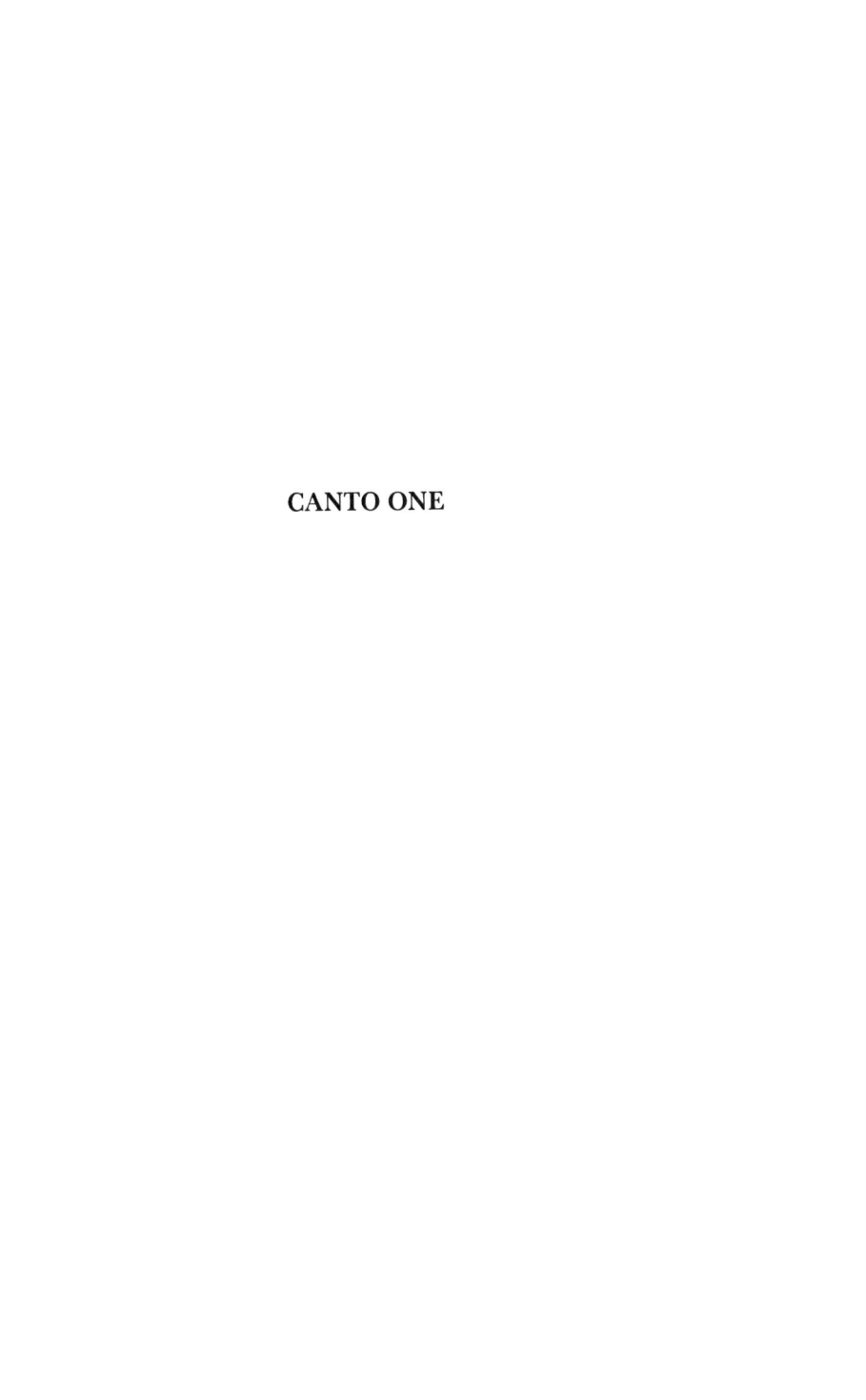

THE PROGRESS OF MAN

I

Peace at last!
Long dreamed of, long prayed for; after ages and epochs
Of creation, behold the clarion of peace is sounding
At last. The wood-pewee and the whip-poor-will
Are singing their lullabies; a breeze is whispering
To the maples; the campfire is glowing in
The twilight; I hear the sticks popping and smell
The burning wood. The smoke is curling upward
Toward heaven (or the "Happy Hunting Ground");
The tawny-skinned Indians are seated naked in a circle
Swapping the stories of their hunting trips,
And night comes on moccasins across the prairie.
No more will the war-whoop be heard,
Nor red paint be smeared on high-cheek bones.
The dream of America, of Europe and of Asia, has it
Come to pass? For Lindbergh, God's own Viking,
And Champion of Peace
Went winging over the sea to Paris.
Then is this not reality?
(Come, who shall say that he is a false prophet
Sent from Beelzebub, this man who answers prayers?)
Hasten Hermes! Be gone at once, winging
The message of peace over all the earth!

II

Behold a world of endless space and darkness,
And cold as any glacier of the Arctic;
How long no living intellect can say;
No song of life had yet begun to swell,

And then there came the Word — the Word of God —
To blend it with His power into forms.
And thus the Word became a brilliant light
Reflecting from a million balls of fire,
Bringing to the universe its warmth,
Swinging around their orbits through the night;
And from the million spheres we know that one
(Whose orbit was determined near the sun)
Had been the dream of God for ages past.
This small sphere cooled and formed a solid mass —
Cooled until on its surface was a film
Of water, like the spheres of falling rain.
The dream went on . . . and in the course of time
(Which has no measure with the Infinite)
This mass, still hot and molten in the center,
Began to boil and cause upheavals at the surface,
Crowding out the water and exposing
A great expanse of land.
Then life! Life! The miracle ineffable,
Pulsating, vibrating life, music and poetry,
The three-in-one, were born upon the land,
And this small planet (so large to human souls)
Was called the Earth. But, was this the origin?
Positively not. Life has its origin with God.
And in the cradle of the sea, endlessly rocking,
Were myriads of simple one-celled forms of life
Responding to the music of the waves
Long, ages long before land appeared;
For all of life emerged from the cradle of the sea.

After millions of years of existence,
Tossing and swaying ceaselessly,

In perfect rhythm and harmony
With the long white lines of advancing foam,
The rustle and thud, the panting sea-breaths —
The living organisms (innumerable in forms)
Amoeba:— single-celled, jelly-like mass,
Without a wall, and sensitive fingers reaching for food;
Flagella:— single-celled with wall, and tail
That whips its way along; Ciliata with tiny hairs
That move it on like a team of racing oarsmen;
Molluscs:— shell-walled, and the fishes
With an inner skeleton, with their many
Changing colors sparkling in the light of day,
Swimming softly through the waters
That encircle this old globe
(Waving to and fro, to and fro,
Their glossy fan-like tails and fins) —
In all their forms they came in peace
To witness great upheavals from the depths.

But who can explain this strange abruptness?
While fish played about the sponges, corals,
And other plant-like forms of odd designs and hues
(Like Persephone within her garden
Before the coming of her gallant lord)
The whole earth trembled with a mighty thunder;
Gigantic mountain peaks arose for miles
Until they towered high above the waves,
Carrying on their backs and rugged sides
A host of fish that failed to find escape.
And as they lay there in the sun,
Suffocating from the dry air, many perished.
While others, finding here and there a pool

Of water in the mud to help sustain them,
Adapted themselves in course of time
To a life upon the land.
Delicate, feather-like gills gave place to lungs.
The fins, each made of many bones
Assembled into one long bone,
And later into several jointed bones
That form the legs of terrestrial vertebrates.
(Who knows but what the plant life from the sea
In time absorbed the green rays from the sun?)
But was the sea that bore all things the origin?
Hardly. For God and life are beginningless and eternal.
It was only the origin of forms conceivable
By the human intellect . . . *Strange new forms
Of plants upon the earth, how wonderful !!*
Breathless, magic, beyond compare the handiwork,
And yet the Great Spirit scanning His vast estate
Could only see the strips of land arising from
The surging blue — strips of land that wore a coat
Of green (the chlorophyl of plants). Then in childish
Fancy, like a poet gloating over his play of words,
He saw on earthly pages the splendor of His script.
And lo, countless millions of vibrating cells
Out of life's unending ocean
Took on myriads of fantastic forms, and
The air was filled with fragrance, music,
And the flutter of youthful wings.
The sea-mountains, which formed the land,
Were leveled off by erosion of streams,
And on this vast surface other majestic peaks
Arose above the clouds into the realm
Of unfailing starlight and sunlight.

The redwoods, those great monarchs of the forest,
With curved branches wrote their messages
Across the deep blue pages of heaven.
Reaching their massive branching roots downward
Into the heart of the earth for inspiration,
Which ascended up through innumerable hollow cells,
Passing through the leaves of many designs into the light
Of dawn. Beeches, graceful elms, oaks unyielding
And scrubby sassafras — all with their messages
Of wonder; the wild flowers, all of different hues
And designs nodding in the breeze as they smiled
Upon the brook — how perfectly constructed!
And in the swamps (perhaps two million years
Before the seed plants, or perhaps living
At the same time as the seed plants)
Were dense growths of the massive coal trees
That bore a brown dust like the ferns
That they might reproduce their kind.
Then, draping the sides of aged cliffs,
Were bracken ferns, rock ferns, cinnamon ferns,
Walking ferns, the mosses and the liverworts;
And moving about through this enchanting paradise
With eyes of wonder and hearts beating contentment
Were these adaptive forms of animal life
With offspring strangely similar to their parents.
Why was there such resemblance? Who knows? Perhaps
This was the secret of their mystery:
The microscopic chromosomes of microscopic cells
Form microscopic embryos that bud and swell,
Developing into animals of individual character
And guided by the Spirit of All Living.
Stand back and see:

The awful tread of God, the touch of His artistic fingers!
Peace and harmony at last! The dream, the dazzling
   dream!
Out of chaos, out of ceaseless cold and darkness,
Out of balls of fire swimming about through space,
Out of a plastic mass of molten rock,
Out of the bowels of the earth, peace and youthful joy!

III

The undistinguished old earth (now a billion
Years in existence) sighed deeply as it spun
Over its well-worn pathway about the sun.
And truly it was the sigh of a sorrowing heart.
On the earth's circumference was the triumph
Of life . . . and then came the dust.
Peace and joy, the dream of all the ages,
And then . . . . . . "Great was the fall thereof." *
Nothing in the world but greed and discord!
The fish that had transformed to reptiles
Arose to be the gigantic dinosaurs, those terrible
Lizards some eighty feet in length,
And weighing forty tons or more, with long tails
And longer necks, reaching to the tops of trees;
With short and heavy trunk and legs
Like the hippopotamus.
Larger ones fed on the leaves and tender grasses,
But the smaller ones had long sharp teeth
And preyed upon the weaker animals.
Triumphantly these rulers of the earth
For millions of years stalked about the swamps,

* Matthew 7:27b

And over the hills, stopping now and then
To crouch down among the coal trees
And listen for approaching prey. So great was their
Dominance that all things cringed in fear before them.
In time the smaller reptiles developed wings,
And made escape by flying through the air.
The larger ones that fed on plants,
And were too large to take flight or run,
Developed heavy armour made of scales
So hard no teeth could ever penetrate;
And so in time these grasping, selfish brutes,
That deposited massive eggs upon the sand
And coldly left them there (without a thought or care)
That when they hatch, the tender offspring shift
For themselves and scrounge for food at the risk
Of being eaten by other creatures; —
These ravenous beasts, with malice coursing
Through their veins, lead to their own destruction.
(Though animals are incapable of moral decision,
Yet the Great Spirit was disappointed that harmony
In all living protoplasm was never shown in animal
Behavior). The whole earth was in tumult, for since
This treacherous age all animal life was in a tense
Struggle for existence. Small salmon devoured the caddis-worm,
The large salmon consumed the small salmon,
As they swam through the swift mountain streams.
The black bear stood knee-deep among the cataracts,
Daylong, night long, anxiously waiting for salmon.
The white ants and other insects destroyed the trees,
Making them fall to the ground and decay.
The birds and snakes destroyed the insects,

And shrikes and other birds-of-prey destroyed
The smaller warblers and the rodents.
All forms of life were fleeing
From the clicking jaws of death.
Then God, as a zealous and determined being,
Like a boy who builds a house of blocks,
And tears it down to build anew,
And thus to build more perfectly, or like
The Master Builder and Creator that He was,
Now exemplifies terrific power.
The power of the upper air, those heights
So treacherous, came into play. For colder
And more brutal than the steel
From the depths that is tempered into swords,
And vicious as the preying carnivores
The great ice-sheets made slow but sure advance.
(Yet no one would have thought it when
The pure white flowers floated down
From a pearl-gray cloud, and then
Fluttered softly like a Grecian gown,
Kissed lightly with a cherub's innocency
The old earth on her throne of destiny, —
No one could possibly discern
That these were harbingers of doom.
Nor would they think these perfect crystals
That capered down in zig-zag lines
Would pile so deep in a solid heap,
And form a mass of solid ice
As irrevocable as a stone wall).
Still onward, onward moved the icy walls.
The frost giant in his wrath consumed the earth,
Cracking and crashing, like the keenest clap of thunder,

Crushing down upon the sides of every
Mountain peak, and pushing countless hills
Before him until at last they broke away —
At last they were cut loose —
These moving mountains from the Arctic peaks,
These colossal streams of ice and snow,
Burying monarchs of the forest alive
Deep beneath their dark debris, killing,
Crushing, devouring with white teeth
All forms of life along their pathway —
These cold and heartless dragons of the North.
All was wasted, and the old earth orbited in
Despair about the sun (or so it seemed).
Great wounds of infection permeated her surface,
And suffering must now be her portion.

IV

The undistinguished old earth,
An insignificant spark of light
Among the millions that fly harmoniously
About God's flaming torch, the sun!
Calm is her glassy surface,
Dripping with condensed humidity
With the serenity of a field of stars,
With quiet eyes sailing through the twilight;
With the serenity of the ashes of a house
Consumed by some unquenchable fire,
Or of the sea when stilled by the hand of Christ.
Then out of the crust of the earth,
The black chaotic mass exposed by melting,
Retreating ice — the feeling of strange warmth,
And the throbbing of new-born life!

Joy emerged, triumphal and beautiful, and shook her
   wings.
Life in all its forms awoke anew,
Took on new light and color, as on the day
Persephone returned to earth.
Life had come, not for a century,
A millenium, an age, nor an epoch,
But God's great measuring stick, eternity.
The soul awoke by the touch of His finger!!
Pray how long was this soul careering
Through countless cells of living protoplasm,
Through differentiated tissues, until at last
It reached the greatest form — the lithesome biped
We call man — and thus the soul of man emerged
Transcending the heights and searching the depths
(The dream of peace and harmony
Cultured within its secret folds)?
Man triumphant over all other forms of life
(After centuries of strategic struggles
With tigers, bears and other beasts of prey),
The divine messenger and creator of all
Things glad and beautiful yet to come,
The hope and incentive of all achievement,
The perfector of an unfinished world, and at last
Designed to wear a crown of glory — This man
Was now to be the master of his role.
In this great soul of man God staked His all;
In him the end of all creation was assured.
For always, always the awful lash of the Great
Disturber, beating on the walls of human hearts —
Hearts of God-Men accompanied by an urgent cry:
   ONWARD! Onward! The world is all before you!!

Arise, O men, with your questing minds —
Minds that are never satisfied.
Then man (taking the human species collectively)
In obedience to an inward urge,
In answer to the call of the sun,
The moon and quiet stars above,
The deep-breathing earth beneath his feet,
And the voice of the wind that passed by
Endlessly careering, began
His quest for greater happiness.
He sought a place of refuge for his wife
And tender brood, found a cave to dwell in
And some wild fruit for their food;
Took the sharp stones from the brook-side,
And, with ingenious mind and hands,
Fashioned tools to meet his needs.
Then as he looked with eyes of wonder
On the sun and moon and stars,
Winds and storms and roaring torrents
(Volcanoes boiling with hot lava
Showering their sparks of fire)
And fancied each held in oblivion
Mysteries immensurable,
He worshipped them with fear and trembling —
Worshipped them and called them gods;
Tried in many ways to please them
That their favor he might gain.
Onward, onward! was his slogan,
Onward through the age of stone,
Digging caves out of the hillside,
Building grass-huts for his home,
Sleeping from the dusk until dawning

Before he had discovered fire.
Fighting wild beasts in the darkness
And winning out because of skill,
Drawing pictures on the cave-walls
With a sure artistic hand,
Telling stories of his hunting
With a merry hunting band.
Fast his kind was multiplying;
Vast communities were formed
And families were joining kindred,
Forming many tribes and clans.
Onward, onward, man advancing!
From age to kindling age he's gone,
Harnessing the beasts-of-burden,
Harnessing each stream that flows,
Traveling far to grassy plains and hills and woodlands,
Seeking pastures for his flocks of sheep
And herds of cattle, and finding ways to till the soil
(First with pointed stick, and then with wooden plow).
On he traveled over continents on backs of horses,
Asses, camels, and sometimes oxen;
And on the streams in little log-hewn boats,
Worshipping the good and evil gods;
Fighting opposing tribes, with keen
Weapons of stone and tempered bronze,
Struggling on and on through wars and pestilence,
And storms and floods: — always with the dream
And hope of some far future paradise
Where peace and harmony abide forever.
Onward, onward, Always onward! Seems that even now
I see him in that ancient day advancing,
Banding with some other tribesmen

On some high secluded mountain, well protected
And far from enemies approaching,
Where he might make a crude fortress
Of defense for himself and all his kindred.
This, perhaps, was the beginning of
The nations yet to come.
Dwellings in these heights were rising
Built of sun-dried brick and straw.
And he built walls about the village
With smooth stones and mud and bricks
Shutting out the lurking robbers,
And destroyers of their peace.
Thus he dwelt in this high village, farming all
The land nearby, and plowing the fields
By use of oxen, threshing his grain
By use of flail, — always seeking
Something better to accomplish every task.
Days passed and even years intervened
Before he starts to realize
The vastness of the world before him
And the endless complications
He must surely overcome
Before the glad fruition of his dream.

V

Civilization arose with its artificial dogmas.
Order ascended out of savagery
(Woe is freedom, for even today her
Pinions are cut and powerless).
The wide-spread peoples of many nations
Depended on each other for food and clothing,
And thus we had commerce among nations.

Cities arose (or city states) and grew rapidly
Among the mountains and the water-fronts
For protection and for trade.
The great Egyptian dynasties arose —
The petty kingdoms in time were joined
To form the two lands of Upper and Lower Egypt,
And later combined into one great Egyptian Empire.
Under a pharaoh of unlimited power thousands
Of slaves were forced to fulfill his
Ingenious plans, and build massive pyramids
Out of two-ton blocks of stone
Quarried from the mountain side,
And carried many miles to make an astounding
Structure, tall as many skyscrapers today;
And under another pharaoh was
A sculptor challenged with his skill,
And together with a band of slaves
To carve out of a pyramid
A life-like image of himself.
The sun-god arose each day at dawning
Out of a state of tranquil dreaming,
Out of the restless Red Sea
Rising like a falcon into the sky,
And blessing all the harvests of the Nile
("Thy dawning is beautiful in the horizon of the sky,
O Loving Aton, Beginning of Life").
The great temples of the gods arose,
And dwelling houses of stone and mud
(Later to crumble to the dust, for what
Nation arises that will not eventually fall?
Yet man, his life beginningless and eternal,
Ever advancing, building, destroying to build anew,

Ever increasing in knowledge, ever seeking to unveil
The mysteries disclosed in every natural object, —
Ever attempts to harness and control
Miraculous forces of the earth and upper air.
Through sorrow, sin, scorn and degradation,
And death ever arises and breathes again
New life and hope with always one great motive:
To help complete this still unfinished world).
Small Phoenician vessels, propelled by an army
Of oarsmen, dared to cross the Red Sea
While Egyptian sailing vessels
(Those single-masted vessels)
Follow them to get the Eastern trade —
Riding the waves like swans,
Catching the wind like gulls
Out on a distant flight,
Those majestic queens of laughing waters.
The Vikings, grim and daring,
With eyes and nerves of steel,
Who lived along the Norseman shores,
And ventured out in their two-mast ships
Far from the sight of land
Had tasted the salty atmosphere —
Had felt the lure of the tide —
And guiding their vessels year on year
Grew drunk with the feel of the rocking keel,
And the swing of the hull they ride.
But there was one who was born of the sea,
Whose pulse was the roll of the waves,
Whose daring would challenge the "Imps of Hell"
And make the devils his slaves.
Leif Ericson "the Lucky", without a hint of fears,

One day, when the tales of sea-dragons were ringing in
His ears, sailed off and onward together with his robust crew.
(No doubt he was a dreamer, dreaming of distant lands.
Perhaps he dreamed of some *new land* —
Of Indian corn and white potatoes,
Of Redskins and of buffaloes,
Of rolling plains and laughing rivers,
Of mountain peaks and redwood forests,
Of rolling mills of bustling industry,
Of youths who lead the world in great discovery;
And possibly one whispered to his soul
Of one bright youth whose smile the world should know,
One future offspring of his who with great wings,
And steady heart and hands would defy
The powers of the upper air, and bridge
The mighty gap between the Old and New,
Offering a peace-pipe for all times).
On and on they sailed at the mercy of wind and wave,
At the mercy of icebergs, of whales and polar bears —
Until at last, after four thousand miles
Of exhausting labor and suffering,
They reached the place they called Vinland.

* * * * * * * * * * *

The old earth turns relentlessly on its axis.
In silent contentment it takes its well ordered
Course about the sun, while on its surface
Man is continually seeking reality.
Tycho Brahe, the sublime author of astronomy,
Out on his beautiful isle,
A paradise for his family,

Watches the heavens through a telescope
Night after night with tireless enthusiasm,
Feeling his way up toward the Infinite
Until at last he discovers a new star —
A planet remote to excite his wonder.
Steadily, steadily he follows its pathway,
And, after patient watching he determines
The course of each of the brighter stars
And calls them all by name
(For they become old friends to him).
John Newton follows Tycho's trail
And, blazing new trails of his own, —
Holding a light aloft for all to see,
Discovers the music and the harmony
That ever exists between the planets of all space —
None ever colliding, nor wandering from their orbits.
All this must greatly aid the navigator,
And bring more light unto the faithful.
O Pioneers, pioneers! — guiding civilization
Into new channels and directing our course,
Blazing trails through the impossible and inconceivable —
Daring to do the things that have not been done before
Despite the scorn and jeers of the multitudes!
Columbus, who sailed to America
And proved a flat world round!
Magellan who circled the rolling sphere,
Battling the storms of the great Pacific!
John McDougall who piloted the Royal William
By steam across the turbulent Atlantic!
And Charles A. Lindbergh who sailed the air
With the silvery "Spirit of St. Louis"
From youthful New York to ancient Paris,

Because of this daring and intrepid deed
In the days of your youth and the stupid age we live in
You have become the greatest of all pioneers,
Moving multitudes of millions with amazement
In Europe, Asia and America!!
You are my endless and triumphal song!

VI

Let us sing the songs of victory
(You sing them; I only sound the key),
Like the Hebrews who sang of bands of warriors,
Their heroes of noble deeds.
This is the song of the great prairie,
The cornhuskers' song and the men of the dairy;
This is the parliamentarian's song
Who brought us the son we'll remember for long;
This is the congressman, pal, and dad,
Who talked and played with his sharp-eyed lad.
This is the modest comrade mother
He claimed for his sweetheart before he had another
(And the peace and harmony he sought for all men
He found in his wonderful marriage to Anne).
This is the song of our hero, the man,
Who to the impossible said, "I can";
More than six feet of energy, more than six feet of grit;
Lips grin at his enemy, and never say, "Quit".
Let us sing of this pioneer, prophet and sage
Who wrote future history page on page!
Let us sing! Let us fling the song on the wing
Of the storm that carried the sleet!
Let it roll from the soul that was fixed on a goal,
And held on until the flight was complete.

FIRST INTERLUDE

Call him the pioneer pilot of the air,
Or the deathless daredevil of discovery and destiny
And possibly the greatest since the dawn
Of human history, but this we know:
The man Lindbergh pressed on in purposeful
Pursuit of the dreams of vibrant youth
That his inward powers might come to flower,
And that his whole being be bathed
In the sunlight of peace and harmony,
Joy and contentment — all of which
Form the substance of perfect love.

CANTO TWO

BOYHOOD DAYS OF LINDBERGH

I

Farmers in dusty shirts and red bandanas
Driving your teams by the puffing engines,
The black smoke curling upward, pitching with great
Energy, golden bundles at steel teeth hungry for straw;
Miners laboring in the world of darkness
With black faces, swinging a pick, stripping the vein
Of coal, loading a car for the donkey to pull,
Or to feed the flames of the President's fireplace;
Factory men and foundry workers feeding the flames for
The liquid iron, molding the parts for a Bellanca plane,
Or a "Spirit of St. Louis";
Bankers with your ringing metal
That drives a doting world to deep distraction, —
You with keen eyes and accurate minds,
Stacking the greenbacks and pecking the adders;
Clergymen, lawyers and neighborhood grocers
Serving the public, serving the masses,
Feeding their spirits, and giving them justice,
Giving them food for the blood in their veins;
Hucksters and venders, peddlers and shiners, —
You, who yell at the folks in the streets,
You who sell 'em the rotten bananas —
"Nanos cheap, nanos cheap, sell 'em cheap"!
You who walk the streets day after day,
Asking construction bosses for a job
(Those big sallow-faced men with cud in one jaw)
Only to have them turn their heads
And say, "Full up today";
You who tidy the house up a bit,

Or stop to nurse an infant in your arms, —
You who rock the cradles of heroes,
And all without acclaim, without ovation —

Turn aside from all your labors,
Forget the puffing of the engines,
The rustle and bustle in the streets —
Forget your fuddled politics, gossip and jazz,
And listen to the song I sing
Which this blundering world shall know;
Not a song that was made by a fool of a poet,
A passionate juggler and fusser with words,
But one molded and tempered by the intrepid man,
By the epochal deed of the Prince of the Air —
The song he took up from the infinite sky
As the wind and the storm were winging it by
(The song of Sir Galahad and Launcelot
Following their comrade through the clouds);
The song that his motor joyfully sings,
As it carries to victory silvery wings.
(Is this a great song? You sing it too!
I'm only sending it on to you.)
Here is the sweet, modest, heavenly mother,
Her head bowed in prayer
That her child may be true and noble and fair,
And here is the bright blue-eyed baby, the princely boy,
Born of a Norseman, yet with Irish hair,
Born of a woman, yet born of the air.
Here is his boyhood; his school days have come.
The slender lad with steady eyes and determined chin
Starts to school, eager to learn all figures will teach him,
Yet loath to study his grammar. Here is the princely

Barefoot boy in his native State of Minnesota,
Land of the sky-tinted waters, wandering with his dog
Over woods and plain, where Red Men hunted and
   fished
In former days; listening to the songs of birds,
Learning their calls, listening to the chiding winds
And watching them move the clouds;
Learning the names of birds and wild flowers,
And where and how birds build their nests
(Who knows but what this energetic boy
Who loved to roam the woods and fields alone
With eager and inquiring mind had watched
The different birds in flight to note the way
Their pinions caught the currents of the air —
Who knows but what he often dreamed that he, too,
Might some day be a pilot of the air?).
Here are the streams where trout are finest (He sees
Them swimming along the bottom in the clear water);
And here is the deep swimming-hole he found.
Ahoy! Look at this on the bank of the lake,
The crude little boat he spent weeks to make!
And here are the oars he used, when he took his dog
Out on long cruises.... At last his boyhood passes,
His muscles wax strong; his mind grows stronger
And more inquisitive; his skillful fingers
Tinker with machinery to see what makes it go.
He takes long walks for hours alone
About the fields and woods and lakes,
And dreams the dream of his career.
Adolescent days pass as well; he leaves
High School and enters college
Working his way in mechanical engineering,

Toiling with a healthy zeal, and
Putting aside all outside pleasures
For the work he loved to do; —
Putting forth an earnest effort, and
Doing more than was required
With determination unparalleled.

II

Behold, the Prince of the Air
Now takes the eagle's throne!
Mercury, so long a god of legends,
Has now become a god of reality.
Lindbergh, as much at home in the air
As sailors on the sea, hears its incessant
Calling, coming over the ceaseless winds
And, heeding quite instinctively
As all his feathered kindred do,
He mounts his lithesome bird and with sensitive
Fingers shifts the sturdy gears, guiding it
Gracefully upward high into the soft breast of
The sky (Lindy then was taking training
For a greater flight to come) until he joined
A flock of flyers in combat against another flock.
Suspended in air, their silver wings basking in
The sun, the pulsing planes collide and crash and whirl.
Lindbergh — caught in the whirling — his mind alert
And muscles tense, ready for any emergency,
Meditated for just a moment to find
What best to do. Then, with parachute in readiness,
He leaped from the cockpit as far from the ship
As he could into the air. Experiencing no sensation
Of falling, he dropped several hundred feet into

The clouds. The parachute had functioned perfectly
Almost as soon as he pulled the rip-cord,
And the risers jerked on his sturdy shoulders.
Like a ghost of the crescent moon in daylight
Appeared the parachute through the clouds.
There Lindy was descending, engulfed in a dense
Gray fog, fighting out the chances for his life,
While he could hear approaching the roaring, circling
Planes . . . Just what could be his fate, and which
Would be the first to reach the ground, the plane or he?
Where would they fall and would they crush
This dauntless heart and mind at last
Or strike him even now while in the air?
What were his thoughts no one could tell,
And yet we know he kept his head, and did all
He could do to save himself from harm.
Who knows, perhaps he even prayed and trusted
In the Infinite to carry him safely to earth?
("For He shall give His angels charge concerning
you; and in their hands they shall bear you up, lest
at any time you dash your foot against a stone"). *
In this adventure, as in many others,
The promise of the psalmist held true.
For as our hero slowly descended
Through the barrier of clouds, and came
In contact with the quiet limpid air,
Fragrant with the verdure of the earth,
He saw the torn and tangled ships crash far below
Him, and burst almost immediately into flames;
And lo, he drifted far away from them,

* Psalm 91:11, 12

Falling safe at last into a field.
Many were his feats of bold adventure,
This man of steady nerves who knew no fear,
But never were they acts of folly.
They only came in his routine of training
Working for a greater destiny — a great fulfillment.
For what else was this strong heart beating?
Think of the night when near to Springfield flying —
The inky clouds, the snowstorm raging; and think of
The cold and the misty darkness; then see
The earnest, serious lad meditating in his cockpit
While the gas-tank of his flying steed
Was burning, burning dry. And see him
Mount up high above the cloud-bank
Thirteen thousand feet in altitude — and then,
Turning loose his "flying horse", leap
With trusty parachute into a sea of chaos.
Calmly adjusting his parachute
To keep away from the falling plane,
And watching keenly for a landing
At last he descended safely!!
And this is the song of the "Prince of the Air",
God's champion of peace.

SECOND INTERLUDE

Your god a dark god, sounding forth his wrath,
His dreadful judgements and disdain by the trembling
Voice of thunder, whose zigzag flashes split
Foreboding clouds asunder; wearily dragging
His long whiskers and matted hair across the ages?
Your god a dark god?
Mine is a bright god. Though filled with the wisdom
Of all the ages, my god is yet a child
With arms chock-full of untarnished dreams,
Casting off many, like bubbles, to fill all space
With planets — all planets with ever more dreams.
Yes, my god is THE GOD ETERNAL, the Lover of all
   souls.
And His arms are full of dreams for each and all —
Dreams that shall remain untarnished if you
Will but let His Spirit guide you into all truth.
He is the Origin and Master of agriculture,
Of sowing and reaping and gathering into barns,
Of art and architecture, of sculpture and
Of music, and even the rat-a-tat-tat of riveting
In all our engineering projects.
He is the Source of all movements in mind and body,
The Source of cybernetics, automation and computation
That in all the forms and patterns of His working
He might speak one language to all people,
The language of creating the beautiful
For the sake of perfect and immeasurable love.
Again, when love comes down at Christmas,
When He shows Himself best of all
As a child, a little shepherd boy born in Bethlehem,

And when darkness passes as the light of heaven overcomes it,
I think I hear Him speaking today, as He spoke
Milleniums ago at the dawn of human consciousness,
And in words like these:— Stand forth, O son of man!
See the world my mind has made, for, like a child
With tops and dolls and sparkling toys, I have been
Toying with the stuff of heaven and earth,
Spinning stars in space with a comet's hair,
Mixing soil and water to blanket the fertile earth
With anchored forests — those multitudes of blessed
Trees that shade and shelter, sustain and lovingly
Protect all of the lesser forms of life.
Yes, in mixing soil and water and watching cells
Unfold, and multiply in innumerable patterns,
I have seen the great abundance of My works.
Everywhere on earth and sea is the crowding of life,
And always in the heart of earth my hidden treasures,
And all of this and more is for you, whom I love.
For in you and your kind have I implanted a part
Of Myself that my life, my mind and spirit be yours
As well. Yet I grew weary of making toys when I
Made you and yours. I said, It is finished this day.
Now you begin where I left off, and may your works
Be even greater than mine. For in all creating
I will never again work alone. I will work through you.
For see, like the Man of Galilee, I am ever young
And joyful. I open my arms to you,
Filled with abundance. In the Son of Mary
I said, I came that you might have life more abundant.
Such abundance is within you as an overflowing
Treasure, and the creative powers of your mind

Are unlimited; for, since in Me all things are possible,
So shall it be in you if you will let My spirit
Guide you into all truth — even like George Carver.
Wherefore, my brother creator, let nothing impossible be.
Traverse every cloud-bank, reach every star;
Penetrate every ocean floor, for no place is ever too far.
But remember the abundance within you is also
Out beyond you, filling all continents and islands,
And deep in all oceans and inland seas. For still
Largely unexplored for treasures and nourishment
Is seventy-one percent of the earth's surface under water.
So push on, my partner, and probe and ponder
To find the base potential yonder in every substance,
In every treasure made by My mind for My
Good pleasure, and for your delight as well.
Reach out, reach in, reach up, reach down, —
Search and research and resound until everything needful
Can be found to prosper every soul the world around.
Devastate every pretense now in hiding. Bring every
Barrier down that separates man from man
Until all souls shall be together one
In love and peace and harmony, and in every tongue
They shall know Me, looking to Me as they ascend
As "Maker, Defender, Redeemer and Friend".

CANTO THREE

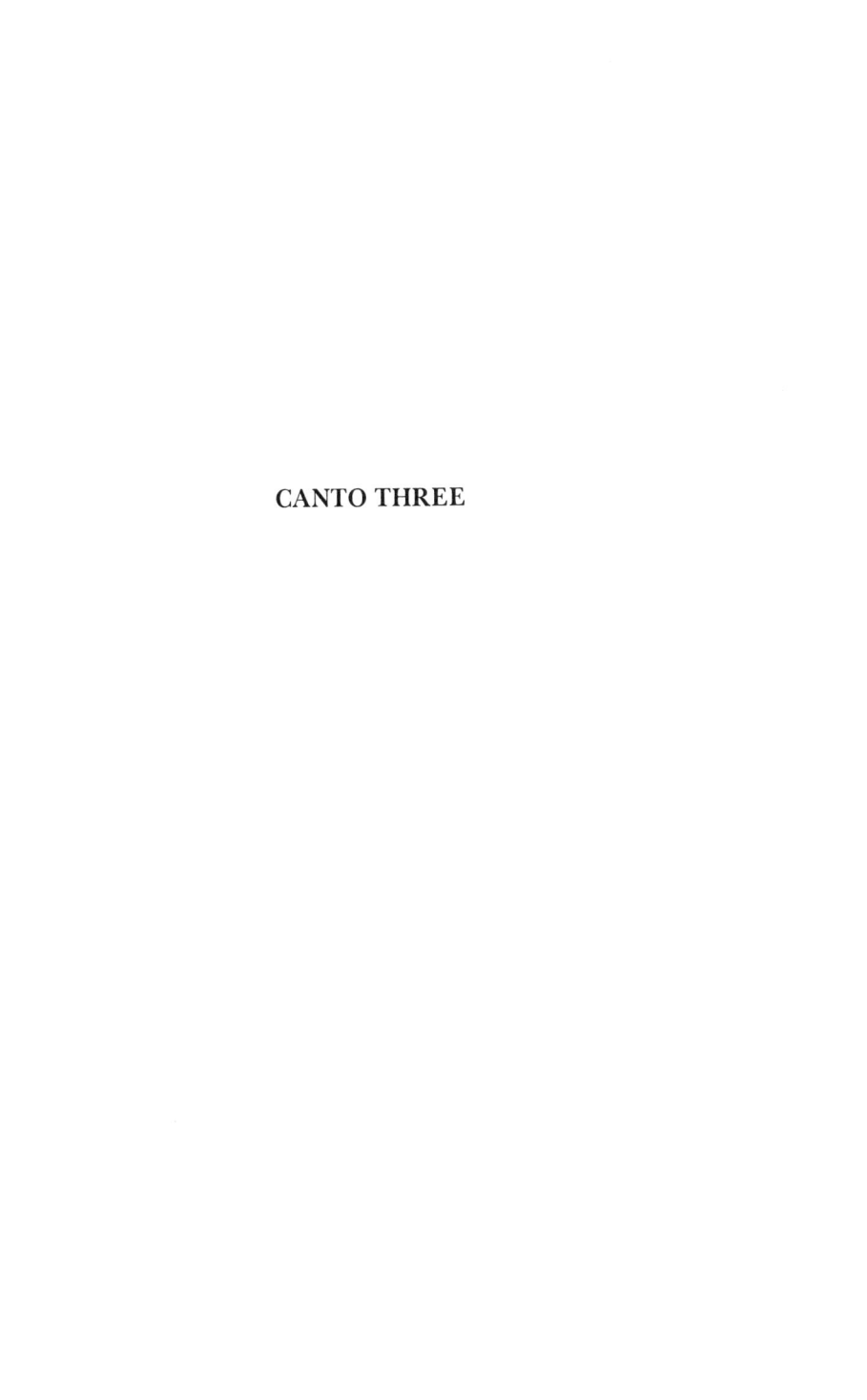

THE PILGRIMAGE OF PEACE

I

Arise! Arise O man,
And dust the cobwebs from your brain-cells!
You who cower about on four feet,
Blundering about with your heads hung, and banging
Your heads against stone walls, only to
Come back and try it all over again
With the dwarfed intelligence of miller-moths
That fly about the street-lamps summer nights —
You, who possess the minds of gods, —
Are you all fools that you should not arise
And learn to stand on two feet?
Are you all fools that you should not profit
By the experience of others or even by your experiences?
You, who are destined to be the crowned kings
Of the earth, triumphal masters of every earthly power,
Bestir yourselves! Pray how long will you trail the dust
With sniffing noses to the ground (For only a straggling
Few, a miserable minority, through all the struggles of
War and crime have kept the dream)?
How long will you be content with paralytic
Minds mimicking the appearances of life?
I see the great continent of North America,
Land of my beloved people, stretched out
Beneath me like a huge green carpet
Covering a deep blue floor of ocean,
Its ragged edges touching three zones.
I see America, beautiful land of our fathers,
The Red Men living content in their youthful,
Undiscovered and unconquered world,

The illimitable wealth of natural resources,
The vast forest regions of millions of acres
Abounding in wild game; myriads of tributaries
To the Mississippi alive with fresh water fish,
Many out-croppings of coal, iron ore,
Silver, gold, copper and oil —
This is America, a great white goddess
Carrying the massive horn of plenty.
I see the great "Fenrirs" of Europe,
France and Spain and England, preying
Upon America, snarling and gnawing at flesh and blood,
Driving the Indians back from the shore, and
The damnable struggle begins. America, the dramatic
Stage of one chaotic war after another; the heroic
Struggle of the Colonies for independence,
The shedding of blood of thousands with gushing wounds,
Chill nights without fuel, or shoes on their feet,
The growing pains and agony of starvation, with frozen
Bleeding feet forging ahead through snow and ice; —
And then, at last, after years of gross
Darkness, grief and torture beyond endurance,
The cry of victory is sounded
Through all the youthful colonies!!
The Colonial fathers and mothers breathe freely
Again of the sweet, untainted breath of peace
As they saunter about their rustic cabins.
A feeling of peace is now continuously with them, and
They rear a new generation, fair and strong,
Only, unwittingly, to cast them into the caldron of hell.
On and on, generations come and go. War and peace
Appear spasmodically; each in turn emerging and
Submerging. Sages make their plans for peace,

Placing many garlands at her feet,
But lo, maudlin rebels, braggarts, babbling ribalds;
Money-grabbers sniffing about the alleys for garbage,
And idiots come and maul them with their folly,
Thinking war the god of silly antics.
Aristocratic Southern planters prosper at
The hands of slavery. They strut about their vast
Estates, looking on their growing fields
With keen appraising eyes; impelling human property
With their whips . . . and all is well.
And yet in time this slavery proves to be
A Frankenstein, and like the mighty Mississippi
It breaks itself free from its channels
Menacing the lives of North and South,
Menacing the life of the United States.
Then A. Lincoln, taking charge of state affairs,
And praying that this monster be controlled
By some godsend, or perchance some peaceful means,
Is drowned by the hideous outcry of war
(Or would be had he dared to wait, for even then
The fires were kindled and burning) and he was forced
To take up arms against his foes —
Foes he would rather be his friends.

A period of peace . . . in which all sages were exultant!
And then the devils of America and all of Europe
Scrap and scramble in rubbish heaps for treasures.
Is this the valiant struggle of Allied Forces
For the sake of democracy? Of all things laughable!!
How can one die for a thing unborn and not
Destroy the very embryo? Who has seen
Democracy barefooted and ragged, walking down

The dusty road? The world's most tragic hour
Approaches; the cohorts of Kaiser Wilhelm approach
With rapid fire and ringing steel . . .
Nearer and nearer they come.
I, a peacemaker, am pierced and stabbed;
I breathe the poisonous gas and liquid fire,
And every inch of my chest and lungs
Are burning with intense pain. No one can
Imagine my agony save Christ, who died upon a cross
(Who said that hell was not on earth?).
My heart stopped beating; my flesh grew cold,
And friends placed me in the ground, covering me
Quite gently with the soil. (But why do you shudder?
This is just the war you were craving for.
Does it not taste well?)
The pressure of loose earth bears down
Upon me. No grass carpets my grave,
And no fair flowers bloom and nod
To speak the thoughts I longed to speak.
Cold and desolate is my grave, and long since
Forgotten by those who pick men off like sparrows;
My grave is in a field of muddy trenches
Where the tread of many armies, with their
Fire-arms, hand-grenades, torpedoes;
Fire and smoke and sword and saber;
With spilling of blood issuing from a thousand
Wounds, and trickling down through the porous soil;
With twisted faces and glaring eyes of men in pain;
With many anxious soldiers bearing
Their wounded "buddies" to safety, with cavalry
Division and heavy artillery firing
Their tanks and rapid machine guns and with

Atrocious murder of women and children at wholesale,
And the destruction of sacred edifices, —
All of which passed and left their weight
Upon me; but not these so much.
I can bear this much of a load without flinching.
Rather it is the tears, the grief and growing
Anxiety, hour by hour and day by day of every
Godly mother in England, France and America,
Who bravely sent her sons to battle
In the face of this increasing death-rate,
That presses down upon me with greatest weight.
To me, who am dead and numb and free from pain —
The pain of this is unbearable. It presses down
Upon me and crushes my bones to powder, and thus
The field of battle is left as cold and
Lifeless as the surface of the moon.
And yet at last the conflict ends . . . with hilarious
Celebrations . . . and soon comes amazing forgetfulness.
(Was this really all they claimed — the last
Global conflict? The end of all wars? Or would there
Be yet another so devastating in its wholesale
Murder and destruction that this would seem only
A family squabble in comparison. And if it come,
Who could save us from this death, from the death
Of all mankind entrapped in all this madness?
Only the deathless spirit of a "LONE EAGLE" who once
Bridged the great Atlantic and thus laid all
The groundwork for space transportation,
And space communications unbelievable —
So that all may see and know of the reigning
Prince of Peace. "And they shall learn war no more.")
Still civilization is in bondage, still fighting

For national survival. O fair triumphal goddess,
Graceful of limb and with throbbing breast,
Standing high on your pedestal, waving your torch
Of freedom across the Atlantic, what do you know of
   freedom?
The curse of slavery is still with us, for men
Are bound to earth and cannot see the stars.

II

The dream passes, and shall continue while there is
Left a soul. See the breathless miracle of blue
Is reaching down invisible hands to you!
Hear the tufted-titmouse down in the gully
In early morning calling, calling!
The graceful elms line the broad-walk;
Their sympathetic branches bow down to form
A natural arch. The breezes pass gently through
The leaves, causing them to quiver timidly.
The farmer takes his team out to the field,
And cultivates his corn in solitude.
Through all of these the dream passes silently,
And men sit beneath the trees deep in thought,
Or sauntering about through cliffs among
The ferns and wet moss are none the less
Receptive and responsive (for peace is their
Immediate goal; not only peace among men,
But between men and the forces of nature).
The yearning unsatisfied soul of Man is ever
Seeking knowledge of his universe
To enlarge and enlighten his world — is ever
Unveiling more and more of
The infinite wonders of God.

But looking back — pioneer planters grew a bumper
Crop of cotton impelling many Negro slaves
To pick the fibers from the seeds.
Then a brilliant man named Eli Whitney,
Probing his brain to solve a problem,
Taking the iron ore from the earth
And smeltering and tempering it into steel,
Assembled a simple smooth contraption —
The cotton-gin that did the work of many
Slaves with amazing rapidity. Robert Fulton invented
The steamboat, blazing the trail of steamship lines
All over this small neighborly world. And puffing,
Hissing, steam-driven locomotives, too, with long
Lines of steel and wooden cars passed first on
Wooden rails and then on steel, passing rapidly
From coast to coast on a vast continent,
Carrying many human beings as passengers, and
Carrying mail (sweet messages of love and friendship),
Carrying great industrial products — these giant
Swift-moving caterpillars became reality.
Benjamin Franklin discovered electricity,
The power that lights all towns and cities,
And most farmsteads all over the world,
Lights the little cottages where families gather
In peaceful, loving conversations, and streets where
Debutantes and celebrities (Lindbergh in their midst)
Pass to the theatre. The newsboy with his small black
Dog, trudging through blinding snow toward home;
Steamboats, those floating cities of the sea;
Electric power that drives the motors of trolley cars,
And most miraculous of all, the carrying of
The human voice by telephone and by radio

All over the world, so our valiant Lindy in his
Devoted way could talk with his radiant mother
Forty-three hundred miles away —
(Who knows but what in the course of time
We'll talk with folks of distant spheres?
Perhaps we'll get a glimpse of Heaven
Or photographs of loved ones who are gone).
The proud mind, continually advancing,
Stripped the most cherished mysteries of nature
And left them all unclothed. The Wright brothers
Risked their lives in their experiments to make
A flying machine that would sail as safely
Through the air as a bird that was born to fly
(Did they dream of the world they created,
Of the innumerable possibilities of travel
And communication, of the peace and joy
Abounding — that they created by their experiments?).
Unwavering the supreme ideal continued
Dominating the souls of a few. The faithful
Scientists in their laboratories, day in
And day out unnoticed by the masses, scrutinized
The world through microscopes and telescopes.
Science was their god; they worshiped him;
They loved him and clung to him as a child does
To its mother.
They found in him the meaning of all
Natural laws and the doctor of all ills
Both spiritually and physically. He was the radiant
Light of eternity to which they turned with eyes
Of wonder. Edison, with an upward gaze toward
Science, reproduced the human voice in a queer
Machine called a phonograph. The flying machine

Ceased to be an experiment; brave air-mail pilots
Flew their planes over continental routes
Daylong, nightlong, winter and summer.
And one lone pilot, who kept the dream,
Quietly prepared to take the flight across
The great Atlantic, while the waiting crowds hurried
About the streets in total ignorance. The game
Was on (No stopping this boy Lindbergh).
With his Wright engine and Ryan monoplane
He flew from San Diego to St. Louis, and on
From there to Roosevelt Field, New York.
America, cherishing again her high ideals
And leaving her muddy plain, was now transformed
Like a white dove with beautiful pinions spread.
Behold, the air was filled with sturdy wings
Of silvery gray, making the bald eagle
Look small and sickly! What triumphal freedom!
For he who breathes of the upper air without
A hint of fear, breathes the *magic breath* of freedom.
The American people, at last enlightened of
The epical flight, came by the thousands in a state
Of breathless excitement "To see the kid off".
The Weather Bureaus reported fair weather,
And all along the Atlantic Coast
Skies were clearing and the sun was tipping
Every curling wave with silver . . . *Three times*
Lindbergh in his cockpit taxied down the runway,
But at last his whirlwind motor lifted the tremendous
Weight high into the air . . . "He is off!
And he'll make it! He'll make it!
To the alluring lights of Le Bourget Field."
The message was wired from coast to coast,

And all over expectant Europe.
Ocean liners caught the message and were asked
To keep a look-out. A prodigious mood had gripped
The whole civilized world as the "Lone Eagle"
Left the field. Forgetful of graft and lusts and crimes
Of every sort, forgetful of the trash and filth
In literature, business and politics — the hopes
And prayers of all the people were with
Colonel Charles Augustus Lindbergh,
The great Archangel of Peace. He was not an American,
A Swede, Frenchman or German, but a great soul of
The ages, a citizen of the world, who even in
These hours of great tension created a World
Brotherhood that shall last for all times.
On and on he sailed while all the people below him
Waited with eager eyes and open mouths.
Following the line of the great circle
Over the land to the north and east
He left all sight of land at Newfoundland.
And then the cold and dismal fog
That formed a bank nearly two miles thick,
The flying below it and above
Ten thousand feet in altitude,
The glaze of ice upon the wings — O who can guess
The half of what this pure untiring soul endured?
*"That's him! That's him! He's circling
the Eiffel Tower! Why don't he come down?
Vive Lindbergh! . . . . . . Vive Lindbergh!*
More than one-hundred thousand persons
Thronged Le Bourget Field as he approached.
He waited for them to clear a place
For him to make his feather-light landing.

The hilarious joy was uncontrollable.
(Though prophets speak from a mountain peak
Of a future world with angels fair
They never dreamed of a world redeemed
By a man who tamed the upper air).
Yet through all the ovations of France, Belgium and
England; through all the tributes, honors, receptions
Of presidents, princes, ambassadors, kings
Lindbergh remained modest and unspoiled —
Representing the flower and fruit of all
That America hopes and dreams.
And here is the man of my greatest song,
The crowning glory of all the heroes and deeds
Of the past, the greatest Dream in the making.
Peace and joy forever shall fill the air from zone
To zone, and from hemisphere to hemisphere.

IN MEMORIAM

Charles Augustus Lindbergh, tall son of a valorous
Viking and child of the Living God,
You, who with the wings of vibrant youth,
Have been lifted and set free from the shackles
Of aged flesh, and passed triumphant through
Heaven's door to be alive forevermore, —
And like all pioneers, prophets and sages,
Have joined the great immortals of the ages; —
As a pilgrim of harmony and peace, I salute you.
I salute you, because you fulfilled the mission
Assigned to you by the Dreamer of all creation;
I salute you because *all alone* you have achieved
More than any other scientist in all
The ages of human existence,
And through it all, by your modesty and sincerity
And your boyish simplicity of life, your words
And manners have done more to mold the minds
And hearts of young idealists than the manners
Of most of the American presidents.
And again, I salute you because now in the spirit
You have taken a higher command than any
You have known among us, and in our hearts
You shall live always.